# *Experiencing*
# THE
# GOODNESS
# OF GOD

## DR. DAN C. HAMMER
## DEENA WILSON

Unless otherwise noted, Scripture quotations are from the New Spirit Filled Life Bible, Thomas Nelson Publishing Company, 2002. Used by permission. All rights reserved.

Printed in the United States of America

First Publication: October 2015

ISBN # 978-1517631383

Ordering Information: danhammerministries@isonrise.org
Ministry information available at www.isonrise.org
Special discounts are available on quantity purchases.
Contact: bookstore@isonrise.org

## WELCOME

Forty days. Numbers 13:25 reveals that the Israelite spies took forty days to explore the Promised Land, a land full of God's goodness. One step at a time, one day at a time, they scouted out this new territory. Two spies, looking through the eyes of faith, found that the land exceeded their best expectations. It was far better than they could ever "ask or hope or think!"

This book invites you to take your own forty-day scouting trip into exploring God's great goodness. One day at a time, one page at a time, you'll be invited to look at your life and world through God's "goodness glasses." Scriptural truths and personal stories will encourage you to discover:

How can I **see**–become aware of–God's goodness?

How can I **receive** God's goodness?

How can I **release** God's amazing goodness to my family, my neighborhood, my world?

You may want to travel solo, taking this 40-day trip on your own. Or you may want to use this devotional together as a couple, family, small group, or church family.

Your bags are packed, your itinerary is ready, and you don't even need any shots for this trip. May your forty-day journey into God's goodness lift your spirit, strengthen your heart and leave you declaring as those faithful spies did: "The land we walked through and scouted out is a good land–very good indeed!" (Numbers 14:7 MSG).

God bless you as you travel!

*This book may be used as a stand-alone devotional or as a companion book to The Goodness of God by Dr. Dan C. Hammer. The Goodness of God offers a closer look and deeper biblical study of God's goodness and is available now.*

# Seeing the Goodness of God

## SEEING THE GOODNESS OF GOD

# Day 1

<u>Psalm 21:3,</u> "For You meet him with the blessings of goodness; You set a crown of pure gold upon his head."

God spoke this verse to me in one of my devotions. He said, "I want to meet you each day with the blessings of My goodness." God wants to meet with us in a very intimate, personal way. Many meetings we attend can seem to be boring. Meeting with God should never be boring. God is a good God, full of goodness and full of life.

In the Scriptures when God met with people it was a life-changing experience. In Exodus chapter three, God met with Moses. Moses was leading the flock of his father-in-law, Jethro, who was the priest of Midian. God called to Moses out of the bush and said, "Moses, Moses!" And Moses' reply was, "Here I am." Moses had to leave the sheep and go stand before Pharaoh. God has a work for us to do just as He did for Moses.

In some of our meetings with God, He will invite us to join Him in His work. He has a special work for you to do. As you are obedient to God, He will show you the work He has for you to do. Remember, He meets you with the blessings of His goodness and He wants to crown you with it.

## REFLECT AND RESPOND

Ask God what work He has for you to do with Him right now. Ask Him if He has any adjustments for you to make. Remember, it's God's work! Receive His good work for you and His assignment.

SEEING THE GOODNESS OF GOD

# Day 2

Psalm 33:5, "He loves righteousness and justice; the earth is full of the goodness of the Lord."

One year after the Civil War ended, the largest producer of paints in the United States was founded in Cleveland, Ohio. Some of their paint cans may be in your garage right now. You'd probably recognize their logo: an inverted can dumping bright red paint on a saturated, dripping world globe. "Cover the Earth!" their slogan proudly proclaims. What Sherwin-Williams marketing execs may not know is that someone else beat them to it, this whole "cover the earth" campaign. Over two thousand years ago, the Holy Spirit whispered to the songsmith of Psalm 33 that the earth is "full of the goodness of the Lord." God's goodness covers the earth.

Imagine it. God hasn't measured out His goodness to us by the dropper or teaspoonful. Talk about going big! Every neighborhood and nation on our globe is being splashed and saturated with His goodness. From the love of families and friends to the beauties of the natural world, from answered prayers to amazing inventions, from the turning of tides and seasons to the turning of hearts and minds, the earth is overflowing with the evidence of a good God. Sometimes we may have to be "goodness detectives" and choose to be intentional about spotting it. But Matthew 5:45 promises it is there. "…He makes His sun rise on the evil and on the good, and sends rain on the just and on the unjust." There's not a single corner or community, house or heart where God isn't willing to pour out His goodness.

My own corner of the world, my home, is being poured on too. There are the bright faces of primroses by my front door, the rare and quick hug from my teenage son, the sound of my elderly mom's voice on the phone. On my bookshelf is my Bible I can freely read. There's hot water for my morning shower, a slice of chocolate pie in my fridge (at least I think it's still there). There are dental bills on my counter, but my tooth no longer aches. There was a difficult family talk last night, but today there's a calm that tells me the air has been cleared. There are dirty clothes heaped in our hamper, but they are evidence of honest work. There are places to go today, people to be cared about, prayers to be prayed that God promises to hear. All reminders of His free-flowing goodness, from His abundant supply that pours but never empties.

When you and I do our morning look in the mirror this week, maybe we can try saying, "Today the earth is full of Your goodness, God." When we slop our coffee, forget an appointment or hit the first frustration of our day (and we all will), maybe we can nudge ourselves into new thinking. *Well, this kind of stinks. But God, Your goodness is still with me*. Whether we feel mad, sad or glad today, maybe we can treat ourselves to this enduring truth: God, Your goodness fills me and my world right now. If we all gave that a try, if we just showed up to see and receive God's goodness, I wonder what might happen? To us and to our world?

## REFLECT AND RESPOND

*God, give me eyes to see Your goodness today. If my day is fairly problem-free, remind me to thank You. If my day is full of challenges, help me be a "goodness detective", still determined to see and praise You for Your many blessings.*

## SEEING THE GOODNESS OF GOD

# Day 3

## LET HIS GOODNESS PASS BEFORE YOU...YOU CAN SEE IT!

Exodus 33:18-19, "And he said, 'Please, show me Your glory.' Then He said, 'I will make all My goodness pass before you, and I will proclaim the name of the Lord before you. I will be gracious to whom I will be gracious, and I will have compassion on whom I will have compassion."

What an incredible experience Moses had with God in Exodus 33. Moses wanted to see the glory of God and so he asked God, "Please show me Your glory." Dare we be bold to ask God the same thing Moses did.

God's answer was fascinating to me. God said, "I will make all My goodness pass before you..." The first thing that God revealed to Moses and had pass by him was His goodness... all of it. I sensed the Lord spoke to my heart and said, "I want My goodness to pass before you and those who will read this book. To be shown My glory begins with My goodness, all of it, passing before you." How has God caused His goodness to pass before you recently? Write down your thoughts, be BOLD and ask God for all of His goodness to pass before you! Ask for more of His goodness! Some of the ways God's goodness has "passed before us" is our salvation, an answer to prayer, a prophetic word coming to pass, someone sending us an encouraging note, or many various things.

## REFLECT AND RESPOND

Stop and think about all the good things that God has done for you over your lifetime. Let them pass before your mind and heart, one at a time. Thank Him for those things! Watch what happens to your heart. Get ready for a lifetime with Him and with His goodness.

SEEING THE GOODNESS OF GOD

# Day 4

Psalm 107:8, "Oh, that men would give thanks to the Lord for His goodness, and for His wonderful works to the children of men!"

I have to admit that I've sometimes yawned in the middle of my prayers and hoped that God wasn't doing the same thing. So my interest was piqued by pastor Mark Batterson's story in his book, *Wild Goose Chase*. He challenged his congregation to try "going right-brain" when they prayed, stirring up some imagination and freshness before they said amen. A good starting point, he suggested, might be to thank God for daily miracles so easily overlooked or taken for granted.

A man in the congregation took Pastor Mark up on the challenge. The holder of a biology degree, he started praying from his own unique science-loving perspective. He began by thanking God for aerobic respiration and for creating mitochondria, each of the amino acids, and his body's bones, ligaments, tendons. With a growing sense of awe, he praised God for glycolysis, for his body's ability to absorb nutrients, for the cochlea in his ears that make enjoying music possible. Once the ball was rolling, he found his thank-yous just kept coming. "I spent the day praying without ceasing!" he emailed Pastor Mark later. "...I literally didn't stop and just consciously kept listing things I was thankful for...While I made dinner, I thanked Him for xylem in the plants I was preparing. I spent a lot of time thanking Him for the molecular properties of water."

I found myself wondering what God may have thought about this creative prayer experiment. If He was in the habit of e-mailing, how might God have responded to the biology-lover's unorthodox display of gratitude? "Dear son," I can imagine Him typing with delight, "you've created quite a buzz here in heaven. I call every star out by name each night; lots of people look up and say thanks. But not many can appreciate what I do with amino acids or something as common as water. Amazing stuff to play with! *Thank you* for noticing. Just love how you see our world!"

You know, there are reasons we love what we uniquely love, be it biology or baseball, Motzart or marscapone. I wonder what would happen if we began thanking God out of the specific loves we find in our hearts? My personal thank-you list would include these kinds of things. Talkative cats with round, inquisitive faces. Dahlias, especially deep red ones. Beautiful words. The way a book's pages feel under my fingertips. The sound of quiet. I'd thank God for the smell of popcorn, pine trees, vanilla. I'd praise Him for the taste of coconut ice cream and dark chocolate. And for the joy of restoring things, be it a friendship or the worn wooden bench by my front door. I'd say thank You for the soothing rhythm of my arms and legs on a long walk. For good talks, girlfriends, times of feeling understood. I'd thank Him for the crinkles around my husband's eyes when he laughs. All these everyday things and more. All-important things.

I wonder. If you thanked God today out of the unique loves in your heart, what would you thank Him for? One thing I can guarantee. You won't be yawning as you pray.

## REFLECT AND RESPOND

Try using some fresh thoughts and new words to praise God today for His goodness to you. No one else is listening. So go ahead, get personal, and thank Him for three or four specific things that matter deeply to you.

## SEEING THE GOODNESS OF GOD

# Day 5

Psalm 27:13, "I would have lost heart, unless I had believed that I would see the goodness of the Lord in the land of the living."

In the world we live in today, it can be easy to lose heart. Strife, war, politics, murders, the stock market and the evening news can be downers. What do I mean—to lose heart? It means to faint or give up. In this psalm, the Psalmist David was making declarations in the midst of challenges. Psalm 27 helps us to hope in the midst of difficulties. God uses it to say, "Take courage. You will see Me and My goodness…don't lose heart…don't faint…don't give up!"

In verse 14 of Psalm 27 David says, "Wait on the Lord; Be of good courage, and He shall strengthen your heart; Wait, I say, on the Lord!" It is wise for us to wait on the Lord when we are tempted to lose heart. As we wait on the Lord, He strengthens our heart. God encourages us. He encourages us to know He will show up. We will see the goodness of the Lord in the land of the living. Remember what Jesus told the disciples in Luke 18:1, "Then He spoke a parable to them, that men always ought to pray and not lose heart." Prayer, waiting on the Lord, is what God tells us to do in these times! You can believe you will see the goodness of the Lord in the land of the living. One more verse that shows this principle is Galatians 6:9, "And let us not grow weary while doing good, for in due season we shall reap if we do not lose heart."

## REFLECT AND RESPOND

*Father, in the name of Jesus Christ, I ask You to help me wait upon You and not lose heart. You will encourage me. I believe I will see Your goodness in the land of the living as I wait on You!*

SEEING THE GOODNESS OF GOD

# Day 6

Nahum 1:7, "The Lord is good, a stronghold in the day of trouble; and He knows those who trust in Him."

In the summer of 2000, I saw the breaking news: a Russian sub, the *Kursk*, had exploded during a naval exercise, sinking quickly into the Barents Sea. The tv blared out unfolding reports: trapped in the wreckage under 330 feet of oily seawater were over a hundred Russian crewmen with little oxygen. Rescue operations were being launched; the clock was ticking.

As I followed the news updates, I struggled with how to pray for these crewmen and their panicked families. I get claustrophobic quickly in tight spaces. And in my twenties, I was pulled under and nearly drowned in a river. So the thought of someone—let alone over a hundred precious someones—being trapped in a cramped space underwater was the stuff of my nightmares. I could hardly bear to think of the *Kursk's* survivors huddling together in the dark, hoping against hope for rescue.

One day as I was praying, a phrase rose and lingered in my mind, "…if I dwell in the uttermost parts of the sea…even there…" I thumbed in my Bible to Psalm 139:7-10 and read again David's beloved song to his always-present God:

Where can I go from Your Spirit?
Or where can I flee from Your presence?
If I ascend into heaven, You are there;
If I make my bed in hell, behold, You are there.
If I take the wings of the morning,
And dwell in the uttermost parts of the sea
Even there Your hand shall lead me,
And Your right hand shall hold me.

Ah, that was it, the direction I was needing. Comfort and peace flooded my heart as I began praying "Even There" prayers for the crewmen of the *Kursk*, "dwelling in the uttermost parts of the sea." *God, even there, in that unthinkable place, I whispered, Your good hand is leading them...even there Your right hand is holding each of them close.* No matter the outcome, I was so sure that God, with goodness deeper than the deepest sea, was right there, moving with love.

Recently I got some personal news, so far off the scale of the *Kursk* tragedy that I hesitate to even make a comparison. It wasn't deadly news, but it was still startling to me, some difficult revelations I didn't want to hear. Some of my hopes and dreams exploded and nose-dived into the deep. On good days, I'm grateful for this news because it is strangely freeing, answers many long-held questions, helps me chart a course for the future. I'm thankful beyond words for compassionate counsel, caring friends and God's promises of hope.

But on hard days, I feel boxed in, made claustrophobic by the changes these insights may bring to me, my family, my future. The air feels a little thick; I have to remind myself to breathe. Sometimes I'm panicky, feeling the watery weight of the unknown pressing down on me. I don't know exactly what answers will look like, or how, or when they will come. I fight the urge to flee, or hide, or scream—or better yet, all three.

But. Eventually, hopefully sooner than later, I do remember what matters most: Who is with me. The Holy Spirit keeps gently, persistently drawing my heart back to the Even There prayers I prayed for others in the summer of 2000. Now, like David, I whisper or cry or shout them for myself. And I remember the truth. My God of goodness is with me and I am being saved.

> Deep and dark cannot contain me.
> Deeper still God's tender care.
> Light and joy will always lead me.
> Love's arms hold me—Even There.

## REFLECT AND RESPOND

Is there an "Even There" situation in your life today?

Cry out to Jesus for the help and comfort you need. He is your stronghold; He will carry you until He rescues you.

SEEING THE GOODNESS OF GOD

# Day 7

Psalm 23:6, "Surely goodness and mercy shall follow me all the days of my life; and I will dwell in the house of the Lord forever."

David's Psalm 23 is one of the most beloved of people of all times around the world. It is a masterpiece. It is about the Lord being our Shepherd! What a wonderful shepherd David was to his sheep. This analogy shows God's heart to us and His people.

I have found the more I look for the goodness of God in life and in the Bible, the more I see it everywhere. Have you ever noticed when you buy a new car, you didn't notice your type of car out on the road very often. But when you buy one, you start to see them "everywhere." God's goodness is like that; the more you become aware of it, the more you see it. I have even felt, as I pursue God, a sense of something sneaking up on me and following me. It is His goodness and mercy following me every day of my life. Watch out, God is sneaking up on you... He's following you with His goodness and mercy every day. Look over your shoulder...His goodness is following you!

Jesus is the Good Shepherd; He is full of goodness. He is good in the way He leads us and manages us as a Shepherd. Jesus loves us! He not only provides for us in this life, but the one to come. David said, "And I will dwell in the house of the Lord forever." God's goodness and mercy will be with you forever. You will dwell with Him forever in His house! What goodness!

## REFLECT AND RESPOND

How have you seen His goodness and mercy following you? Thank God for it in prayer today.

SEEING THE GOODNESS OF GOD

# Day 8

Psalm 119:68, "You are good, and do good; teach me Your statutes."

Interesting, what I read about Gillette's new low-cost razor for India. It seemed promising enough. The company test-marketed it here in the U.S., so why, when the razor debuted in India, was it such a flop? Believe it or not, company executives went jetting over to India to find out, spending hours watching men shave. (Now, there's an assignment for you!)

Guess what they saw? Few bathrooms. Often no electricity, no lights. No mirrors. And most importantly, no running water—the best way to rinse out a clogged razor. For most Indian men, shaving meant squatting on the floor at dawn with just their razor and a bowl of water. What an eye-opener for Gillette. Not having grasped some of the basic realities of life in rural India, it was back to the drawing board for a safer razor, less likely to clog or nick.

Basic realities. Ordinary life. The thought occurs to me that Jesus was no stranger to these. Knowing mankind inside and out, He still did something so much more than designing a patch for our pain from a safe distance. He even did more than jetting into our world to spend hours watching—up-close and personal—as we did life. Instead, He did life Himself alongside us. He stepped down into time, history, a culture, a family. He had an address, a birthday, a belly button, a breakable body. He had fingerprints, friends, tears, habits, scars, family stories, His own way of laughing. And He had good questions too: "What do you want Me to do for you?" "Who do you say that I am?" "Do you want to be healed"? He didn't assume; He asked.

"This High Priest of ours understands our weaknesses," reveals Hebrews 4:15, "For He faced all of the same testings we do, yet He did not sin" (NLT). There was no Gillette-like miscalculation in Jesus about what it was to be human. No detached analysis, no misunderstanding. He knew how it felt to hammer His own thumb at the carpenter's bench, to have His own heart broken by a friend's betrayal, to dance to His own favorite song at a wedding, to have His own skin ripped by a Roman whip. He knew life deep into its corners, tasted and tested it, held every authentic claim on the experience of being alive. When you think about it, Jesus squatted down in the darkness of our broken world with us and understood fully what we were without—living water and light. And a mirror to see who we really are. Whose we are.

Hebrews 4:16 invites, "So let us come boldly to the throne of our gracious God. There we will receive His mercy and we will find grace to help us when we need it most"(NLT). Sometimes I ask myself, does Jesus really understand my world? Does He "get" my pain? Can I throw the weight of my life, all my anxieties and hopes, on Him today? Can Jesus teach me how to do this life? For me the answer is yes.

Even though He probably never shaved.

## REFLECT AND RESPOND

Is there a part of your life you think Jesus has trouble understanding? Can you try talking to Him about it today as you might to a trusted friend who has experienced the same thing?

An amazing part of His goodness? He really does "get it."

SEEING THE GOODNESS OF GOD

# Day 9

Romans 2:4, "Or do you despise the riches of His goodness, forbearance, and longsuffering, not knowing that the goodness of God leads you to repentance?"

God's goodness led me to repent for my sins on August 11, 1975 in Appleton, Wisconsin at my grandparent's house. I was struggling emotionally, mentally and spiritually. God helped me to change my mind, open my heart to Him and the Gospel of Jesus Christ. I turned from my sin and asked Jesus Christ to come into my heart and life and become my Lord and Savior. God's goodness filled my heart.

The word for *repent* in the Greek is *metanoia*, which means "a change of mind." God's goodness causes conviction by the Holy Spirit to realize we are going the wrong way and doing the wrong thing. At that point we "change our mind" and go God's way and do the right thing. 2 Corinthians 7:10 says, "For godly sorrow produces repentance leading to salvation, not to be regretted; but the sorrow of the world produces death." Godly sorrow leads us to salvation, but the world's sorrow produces death. Some are only sorrowful because they got caught sinning.

God in His goodness causes us to think His thoughts. His thoughts are true. The enemy tries to flood our mind with his thoughts, which are lies. So God in His goodness leads us to repent, "change our mind," and to think His thoughts about God, ourselves and others. All sin problems are relationship problems that deal with our relationship with God, ourselves and others. Let God "change your mind" to think like He does. Yes, let's get out of our minds and into His mind.

Remember: God's thoughts are not like our thoughts. They are way better! Isaiah 55:8,9 says, "For My thoughts are not your thoughts, nor are your ways My ways,' says the Lord. 'For as the heavens are higher than the earth, so are My ways higher than your ways, and My thoughts than your thoughts.'" His thoughts and ways are so much higher. His thoughts can "blow our minds."

## REFLECT AND RESPOND

Ask God if there is anything you need to repent of, "change your mind" and ask Him in His goodness to lead you to think like He does about the issue!

SEEING THE GOODNESS OF GOD

# Day 10

Psalm 34:8, "Oh, taste and see that the Lord is good; blessed is the man who trusts in Him."

Writer Jan Karon will tell you that almost anyone is willing to talk freely about their favorite foods. She took the time to pull together a "favorites" list from her friends and dinner guests. It included meatballs, mashed potatoes and lingonberries for a Norwegian friend craving the comfort food of her heritage. Fig Newton cookies for the man who remembered eating them as a little boy with his dad. And Jan's agent, a fellow food-lover and elegant hostess, revealed her favorite meal: "a lovely slice of foie gras...a gorgeous salad from my own garden...and a Maine wild blueberry pie with vanilla ice cream." All I can say is yum. And remind me—what is foie gras?

I'm all for sinking my teeth into mashed potatoes and wild blueberry pie, but how on earth do I "taste" God as Psalm 34 invites? God is a living Spirit, not a salad or a salami. He's a heavenly Father, not a French roll or a Fig Newton. But wait. I'm thinking that the wording of Psalm 34:8 reads something like an invitation to a tasting party: *Taste and see that the Lord is good.* And the second part of that verse is like a map to the party site: *Blessed is the man (or woman) who trusts in Him.* The directions to the party—the route to tasting God's goodness—is to trust

Him. You want to get your lips around something fantastically delicious today? Sink your teeth into God in some new way. Be brave, try a taste, chew, swallow. You like?

For a "tasting sample", consider this. Is there a relationship you've been avoiding? How about taking some small, sacrificial step toward that person? Swallow and just do it. That's a little "bite" of God.

Or is there a habit you've been longing to change? Today is as good a day as any to ask God to help you start a healthier pattern.

Is there a dream you've been neglecting? Can you buy some art pencils, sign up for that class, check out ticket prices?

Do you have a gnawing worry? Right now can you transform that anxious thought into a declaration of trust in God? Can you thank Him for His good answer even before anything changes?

You get the idea. Granted, we're talking about some risk here, but none of us ever tasted anything just by eyeballing it, sniffing it, poking it, or putting it in our ear, right? (Well, maybe we *did* taste that way as kids.) But tasting for grown-ups means committing ourselves to at least a try, an honest bite, and a swallow. And God promises that bite of Him is going to be tasty. We'll be coming back for seconds because He's so good. Guaranteed.

Favorite foods for me? Chopped sirloin done medium with grilled mushrooms and onions. Cherry pie with incredibly flaky crust. Warm, crisp tortilla chips with lime. Ice-cold watermelon. Chocolate cake so dense that just one bite is impossible. And oh, the list goes on…

## REFLECT AND RESPOND

*Lord, help me be willing to take one risk today, make one change, step outside my comfort zone and try a fresh direction. Show me what this "bite" of You might be, so that today I can taste Your goodness in a new way.*

SEEING THE GOODNESS OF GOD

# Day 11

Psalm 52:1, "Why do you boast in evil, O mighty man? The goodness of God endures continually."

Psalm 52 is written by David. This was his contemplation when Doeg the Edomite went and told Saul that David had gone to the house of Ahimelech. It shows the battle of evil versus good. Doeg's tongue in verse two caused innocent godly priests to be killed.

1 Samuel 22:9-23 tells the story that relates to this psalm. Doeg the Edomite was set over the servants of Saul and said in 1 Samuel 22:9,10, "…I saw the son of Jesse going to Nob, to Ahimelech the son of Ahitub. And he inquired of the Lord for him, gave him provisions, and gave him the sword of Goliath the Philistine." David was running from Saul at this time. So Saul had Doeg the Edomite kill 85 priests with the sword and then killed men, women, children, nursing infants, oxen, donkeys and sheep in the city of Nob. They were innocent of wrongdoing. Evil brings destruction.

David in Psalm 52 says, "Why do you boast in evil, O mighty man?" The goodness of God endures continually, even in the midst of evil. God's goodness gives life to people! In verse three of Psalm 52 David says, "You love evil more than good, lying rather than speaking righteousness." In verse five and six, David says, "God shall likewise destroy you forever; He shall take you away, and pluck you out of your dwelling place, and uproot you from the land of the living. Selah.

The righteous also shall see and fear, and shall laugh at him…" God's goodness continues forever! We overcome evil by doing good!! We will see God's goodness forever, because it endures continually. We can continue to expect to see God's goodness over and over. We will see God's judgment on evil and fear the Lord.

Let's see God's goodness in the midst of evil. Let's overcome evil with good. What goodness do we see we can bring into the midst of evil circumstances?

## REFLECT AND RESPOND

Goodness triumphs over evil! Is there an evil situation where you see how God's goodness could come into it and make a difference? Pray about it.

SEEING THE GOODNESS OF GOD

# Day 12

Psalm 107:9, "For He satisfies the longing soul, and fills the hungry soul with goodness."

It's a whole new world. We dropped in on a family friend recently. He's pursuing a Ph.D. in robotic nursing and lives ten minutes away from us, but he's "attending" the University of Arizona. "See? There I am." On his opened laptop, we could see, in real time, his "robotic self", a rolling contraption with a screen for a head. At the click of a mouse, he sent the robot gliding through the hallways on the UA campus as we watched. "This is how I interview professors, do my research." Wow.

Not long ago I saw a documentary on the future of AI, artificial intelligence, that branch of science focused on making computers behave more and more like humans. In a nutshell, the program suggested that at some future tipping point in history, exploding technology will inevitably outsmart us. Frankly, when I hear about things like an oblivious GPS-led driver steering blithely into a lake, I wonder if this has already happened.

As I watched the AI program, I was struck by one scholar being interviewed. A slight, balding man with a contemplative demeanor and thick glasses, he seemed almost scarily brilliant. As he spoke about the promise of artificial intelligence, he sounded hopeful—but somehow also deeply sad. As the special rolled on, filled with head-spinning concepts—computer and human brain interfaces, living in virtual realities, cyborgs and much more—I began noticing something else about this man. He was heartbroken about his dead father.

He told the interviewer that his dad, a gifted musician, composer and conductor, had been a mysterious presence in his childhood. When an early heart attack weakened him, he had kept his musical career alive by working from home. It was only then that he became, too briefly, something of a confidant and mentor to his then-teenage son. He died an early death. Filmed standing at his dad's grave, wiping his eyes, this accomplished man of the mind confessed wistfully that he always felt better standing there at the gravesite, but he really didn't know why.

By the close of the program something else was abundantly clear. His passion for artificial intelligence was driven partially by his longing to somehow reach beyond the grave and retrieve his lost dad. He was collecting and cataloguing mountains of data about him: photos, letters, original compositions, genealogy records, family stories. He hoped aloud that maybe technology could someday replicate something or someone very close to the father who had slipped away before he could really know him. I watched and thought, *Oh, the inescapable longings of the human heart*. Whether we have the attention span of a gnat or the very long intellectual reach of a scholar and researcher, our hearts are fashioned alike.

What does Jesus have to offer this gifted man, this grieving son, with a universe of concepts in his head and a universal ache in his heart? This promise from God, the ultimate Father: *I'll never leave you. My love can never be lost. Son, will you let Me heal you and satisfy your soul?* What a wonder, that anyone, anywhere, anytime, of any IQ, receives this very same invitation. For all of us who will let ourselves fall into God's embrace, there is no "maybe someday", no waiting for healing to finally come to us. The future is now.

## REFLECT AND RESPOND

Is there a hunger in your soul? Can you tell God what you're longing for?

*God, thank You that Your goodness is deeper than any hunger or hole in my soul. By faith, I ask You to begin healing and filing me today so I can walk in the wholeness You have for me.*

RECEIVING THE GOODNESS OF GOD

# Day 13

Hosea 3:5, "Afterward the children of Israel shall return and seek the Lord their God and David their king. They shall fear the Lord and His goodness in the latter days."

Hosea is an incredible book and story of God's love and mercy. Hosea is called by God to marry a woman who is unfaithful to him. His wife lives an immoral lifestyle. God's love and goodness are so incredible. In this story, God likens Hosea and his wife to God and Israel. Israel wandered from God. But God's love and goodness are so powerful. He loves the unlovely. He is good to those who deserve no goodness! He is a good God!! Israel has turned from God.

But Hosea declares that they, "...shall return and seek the Lord their God..." He goes on to say in this passage, "They shall fear the Lord and His goodness in the latter days." The word *fear* in this passage is interesting. "Fear, *pachad* (pah-chad); Strong's #6342: To be startled, to tremble; to stand in awe; to revere, or fear; be amazed. *Pachad* concerns a person's reaction to something sudden and startling to the point of trembling. The verb appears in the Bible 24 times. The noun pachad, which refers to something dreadful and awe-producing, occurs more than 40 times. Hosea is saying that Israel will tremble because of God's startling, sudden, amazing goodness showered upon them in the latter days!"[1] God wants to startle us with His goodness to the point of producing awe in us of Him. Jesus wants to startle us with His goodness.

I experienced this personally. One of our members, Dr. Tom Giesecke, called the church office to say two men would be stopping by to see me. When our receptionist told me, I was puzzled about who they might be. To my surprise, one was Dick Leggatt, the president of Derek Prince Ministries. I'd heard his name, but had never met him. Derek Prince, the great Bible teacher, was a hero of mine. I love his books and teaching.

Dick said that Tom had told him about me and our church. Then he proceeded to offer me and the church an incredible gift: Derek Prince's library of books, DVDs, CDs and audio broadcasts. I began weeping, startled by the goodness of God. What a special gift from God and Dick! It produced awe in me—and a greater fear of the Lord.

Obviously, Jesus is the goodness that will startle Israel in the latter days as they return to the Lord! I was startled by God's goodness when He saved and delivered me. I am so thankful for God's goodness shown to me in Jesus Christ.

## REFLECT AND RESPOND

Are you ready to be startled by God's goodness? Ask God to help you see the goodness of God that Hosea spoke about to Israel! Get ready to receive!!

---

1 The Spirit-Filled Life Bible, (NKJV), Thomas Nelson, Nashville, TN, Jack Hayford, General Editor, (©2002), pg. 1147.

SEEING THE GOODNESS OF GOD

# Day 14

Psalm 65:4, "Blessed is the man You choose, and cause to approach You, that he may dwell in Your courts. We shall be satisfied with the goodness of Your house…"

My naturopath and I were tweaking my diet. Was I getting enough calcium for bone health? Vitamin D? Dark green leafy vegetables? I had questions for her. How many servings of nuts were too many?  How many times a week did I need to eat fish for the healthy fats? On we talked, quantifying all sorts of things, and then we discussed oatmeal. You have to understand, oatmeal and I are pretty tight friends. It's high on my list of go-to comfort foods, especially on chilly, drippy days. "So, oatmeal? How much?" I asked. My pen hovered over my notes. My doctor smiled, relaxed back in her chair, and proclaimed, "To satisfaction!"

My little oatmeal-loving soul sighed with relief and pleasure. To satisfaction!  Not one-half cup or so many times a week or only if combined with protein. I could eat oatmeal with abandon, without limitation—as much and as often as my heart desired. If you despise oatmeal, this is nearly impossible to understand. So just substitute something you really like—say, cheese tortellini or hot fudge sundaes—and imagine eating that to blissful satisfaction. Truthfully, even I don't want oatmeal more than a few times a week, but it was the principle of the thing, the freedom, the easy way my doctor laughed and waved her hand. It was as if she was saying, "Hey, no worries. Have at it!"

Psalm 65:4 promises, "...We shall be satisfied with the goodness of Your (God's) house." When it comes to His goodness, it's as if God laughs and says, "Hey, have at it!" Of all the names He assigns to Himself—Savior, Healer, Teacher, Counselor, Protector, and much more—there is one implied name that's easy to miss: Satisfier. Psalm 145:16 reveals, "You open Your hand and fill the desire of every living thing."

It only takes a quick peek at nature to see the extravagance of the Satisfier-Creator. God could have dusted the universe with a mere sprinkle of stars and made every sunrise and sunset identical. He could have populated the earth with matching people all six feet tall with blue eyes, brown skin and outgoing personalities. He could have created just two or three musical notes, splashed all trees the same shade of green, limited Himself to fashioning three basic flowers. He could have skipped designing summer lightning, laughter, the polka dots on a ladybug. He could have stepped back and called it good after creating one mountain range, a couple birdsongs, a season or two. But He just wasn't satisfied with a world like that.

And it only takes a quick peek in the Bible to see God, the generous Satisfier, in action. When the wine ran out at that local wedding, Jesus could have created a few extra glasses of basic table wine for each guest, just enough to squeak through the party SOS. Instead He crafted six (count 'em) 20 to 30 gallon jars of eyebrow-raising, premium wine (John 2:1-12).

And consider this. Jesus, the creator of oceans, sat hot and thirsty on the edge of a well and chatted with the village outcast. He could have offered her a few drops of hope, like, "Maybe with time and a lot of effort, you can get your life together. Someday." Instead he looked into the deep well of her eyes and saw the bottom of her pain. He said quietly, "I know. About your five husbands? Will you let Me show you how to never thirst again?" (John 4:4-30).

So keeping in mind the devoted Satisfier that God is, do you need wisdom today? "If you want to know what God wants you to do, ask Him, and He will gladly tell you, for He is always ready to give a bountiful supply of wisdom to all who ask Him…"(James 1:5 TLB).

Do you need hope, joy, peace? "Now may the God of hope fill you with all joy and peace in believing, that you may abound in hope by the power of the Holy Spirit" (Romans 15:13).

Or life? "…My purpose is to give life in all its fullness." (John 10:10 TLB).

Your Satisfier, the God of goodness, is as close as a prayer. Expect His abundant goodness and receive—to satisfaction!

## REFLECT AND RESPOND

*God, You are my great Satisfier. Your goodness is deeper, higher and wider than any need I have. Thank You for filling me to overflowing with Your goodness today.*

# Receiving the Goodness of God

RECEIVING THE GOODNESS OF GOD

# Day 15

Psalm 65:11, "You crown the year with Your goodness, and Your paths drip with abundance."

God wants "to meet us with the blessings of His goodness" in Psalm 21:3. The verse also says, "You set a crown of pure gold upon his head." If you look for God to meet you with the blessings of His goodness, you will see His goodness.

In Psalm 65:11, God speaks through the Psalmist David and says, "You crown the year with Your goodness." He not only meets us with His blessings day by day, but He crowns our "year" with goodness. God wants to crown you with goodness this year.

In verse 11 it also says (speaking about God), "And Your paths drip with abundance." I have lived my whole life in the Pacific Northwest. I am used to rain, and I even like it! I used to love to walk outside with an umbrella when I was little and listen to the rain. I am used to rain drops and rain drips. God wants to rain His goodness upon you! May I make a suggestion? Don't put up your "umbrella"…let God soak you with His goodness! One of the ways God shows us His goodness is by dripping on us with His abundance. God is the God of abundance. In Ephesians 3:20

it says, "Now to Him who is able to do exceedingly abundantly above all that we ask or think, according to the power that works in us." Wow! Let your imagination run wild and God is able to do exceedingly, abundantly above all you can ask or think according to the power of God that works in you!

Watch out for His goodness abundance-drips. As a matter of fact, He might start to rain goodness on you! Watch.

## REFLECT AND RESPOND

*Father, in Jesus' name, I thank You for covering my year with Your goodness. Thank You that Your paths of abundance are dripping all over and around me!*

RECEIVING THE GOODNESS OF GOD

# Day 16

Psalm 52:1, "...The goodness of God endures continually."

The legends say that it passed through the hands of Joseph of Arimethea, King Arthur, the Vikings, assorted monks, French knights, the Nazis, Indiana Jones and others. The myths and mystery abound. And now, according to two historians, the Holy Grail has finally been found. Again. It is safe and secure, they claim, and has been sitting right under our unsuspecting noses for hundreds of years. Who knew?

Oh, that sought-after, elusive cup that Jesus supposedly sipped from at the Last Supper! In spring of 2014, crowds swarmed into a church in northern Spain for a glimpse of it. The historians are claiming that the cup has been at the church since the 11th century. But it has been in hiding, tucked inside another chalice belonging to a Spanish princess. An undiscovered treasure, hidden in plain view.

Recently my friend began telling me a story about the cup of Jesus, and of course, my ears perked up. It turned out that she wasn't talking about the literal Holy Grail, but about something different, something more. She heard the story years ago from a local counselor, Claude McCoy. Unfortunately, the trail of origin blurs there, so I can't give credit where credit is due.

"So when we're born," my friend began, "it's as if we each get our own personal 'cup'. All our lives, our cup is being emptied and filled. We're loved, we're valued, we have successes: our cup fills. We get hurt, tired, discouraged: our cup spills." I nodded. "When we have needs and wants," she said, "others pour from their cups to help fill ours. When others need us, we pour from our cup to fill theirs. Right?" I was with her so far, on this reciprocal emptying and filling.

"But then we're born again," she went on, and I sensed that the story was warming up. "And we get a gift. A second cup—the cup of Jesus." My story-loving heart whirled ahead to what the cup of Jesus might be like or look like. "His cup is always there for us, even when people aren't or can't be. Always ready to fill us up again." She smiled. "And no matter how much His cup pours out? Well, it's still always full."

I sank back on her couch and studied the air. Always there for me. Always ready. Always full. That's a lot of always. I've loved Jesus for much of my life. But…somewhere deep beneath my ribs, I was feeling an ache, a longing for more from the always-available cup of Jesus.

I need His cup when circumstances disappoint me. When I'm excluded from the group. When I feel like a failure as a mom. When my body aches or my head throbs. When my gifts don't look as shiny or needed as someone else's. I need His cup when my life has more questions than answers. When dearly-loved people leave me and difficult people stick around and multiply. I need His cup when I don't measure up. When the bills pile up. When I wonder if God will really show up. When I'm scared of my future or dogged by my past. Oh Jesus, help this girl. I need Your cup.

The prophet in Isaiah 55:1 invites you and me to a long, cool drink from the cup of Jesus. "Say there, is anyone thirsty? Come and drink, even if you have no money…it's all free" (TLB). And 2 Corinthians 1:20 echoes with good news for the parched in heart, "For all the promises of God in Him are yea and in Him amen to the glory of God…" (KJV). Promises of peace. Protection. Healing. Hope. If the cup of Jesus really was a physical cup, maybe I would hold it up to the light, turning it over and over again in my hands, and see that it was beautifully engraved from top to bottom with the word yes. Yes to every promise of a good God.

The real cup of Jesus? It isn't some dusty relic sitting on display in a church in northern Spain. It's Jesus Himself, real, alive and present—with us, in us, and for us. Every day and always. We drink Him up—and live.

## REFLECT AND RESPOND

In what area of your life do you need a drink from the cup of Jesus today? Will you bring Him that need and let Him comfort and fill you with His goodness?

Can you offer at least one person today a "drink" of encouragement or hope?

RECEIVING THE GOODNESS OF GOD

# Day 17

Psalm 34:8, "Oh, taste and see that the Lord is good…"

This psalm was written by David as he pretended madness before Abimelech. Sometimes, like David, in our strangest circumstances in life we taste the goodness of God. David had fled from Saul and he was now seeking shelter in the land of the Philistines. This is the backdrop of Psalm 34.

When you taste and see how good God's goodness is, it is sweet! We can taste His goodness and see His goodness. 1 Peter 2:3 says, "…if indeed you have tasted that the Lord is gracious." In the worst and strangest times in your life, you can taste and see that the Lord is good!

It is great to smell food, but it's certainly a lot better to taste it! As you and I swallow food, we ingest it and savor its good taste. I love a barbecued steak; grilled to perfection, full of its great juices. I love banana cream pie. Thinking about it makes me want a steak and a slice of my wife's banana cream pie. As I think about God's goodness, it makes me want to taste His presence and goodness. I am "hungry" for God and want to taste His presence. Do you hunger to taste His goodness?

Why not try the taste test? The only way you can really know God's goodness is to take the taste test. My wife and I go to

Costco and as we are shopping they have people who have samples of goods that they want you to taste. It is fun to try these new foods. Some I like and some I don't. The only way I know if I will like it is by tasting it! You have to taste it for yourself. I can tell you how good God tastes to me, but the only way you know for sure is to taste it yourself. Ask God to show you His goodness; it's all around you.

## REFLECT AND RESPOND

Go ahead and take a "bite" of God's presence. Once you have a taste of His goodness, nothing else will satisfy! Lord, show me Your goodness in new ways and depths today!

RECEIVING THE GOODNESS OF GOD

# Day 18

Romans 2:4, "Or do you despise the riches of His goodness, forbearance, and longsuffering, not knowing that the goodness of God leads you to repentance?"

I think that ancient Greek storyteller, Aesop, had it right when he came up with the fable of the wind and the sun. Maybe you know how the story goes. The wind and sun had a difference of opinion over the definition of true strength. Spotting a traveler coming down the road, the sun had a brilliant idea. He proposed that whoever could convince the traveler to remove his coat would be considered strongest. The sun stepped behind a cloud as the wind began to blow. Harder and harder he blew, but the fiercer the gusts, the tighter the traveler gripped his coat around him. Finally the wind gave up in despair. Then the sun slipped out and began to gently warm the morning air. Within minutes, the traveler was whistling as he eagerly pulled off his coat.

Have you ever hit situations where you've been just like the wind, all bluster and blow? Let me guess how that worked out for you. Who among us hasn't been there? Think teenagers, toddlers, time crunches, tensions. Ever try bossing around a spouse or co-worker? Demanding time from a friend? Bullying a struggling heart toward faith? It's not hard to guess what happens. Hello, pushback! Funny isn't it, how a show of force just rolls out the welcome mat for resistance? Tempers flare. Bottlenecks and battles begin. Too often, relation-ships tear in the wind. Imitating the wind seems the perfect way to blow it.

But Romans 2:4 shows that God models a different way for us. He uses His goodness to draw us to a change of heart. He uses His strength to gently insist that our choices are ours alone to manage. Rather than hunting us down to rope us into relationship with Him, He patiently pursues us. Rather than barking in our faces like a drill sergeant, the God who fashioned galaxies pulls out a chair and says, "Come on, let's talk this over together." Rather than threatening, "Toe the line now—or else", the One who times our every heartbeat invites us to consider. Do we really choose to love Him? Or not? And "not" is an option He'll grieve, but accept as our answer for now. Though He'll never end His passionate pursuit of our hearts.

It's pretty amazing, isn't it, that every day as we travel this life, God simply comes and shines on us with goodness, with the warmth of all He is. And He stays the course until our resistance is melting like wax and any pushback is in a puddle. That's when we just can't wait to peel off whatever old, heavy coat of sin or guilt is weighing us down. It's what we most want to do.

## REFLECT AND RESPOND

Has God been "shining" on you in some area of your life to persuade you to lay down a habit, belief, behavior or way of relating?

Are you being the sun or the wind with those in your circle of influence?

RECEIVING THE GOODNESS OF GOD

# Day 19

1 Chronicles 17:26, "And now, Lord, You are God, and have promised this goodness to Your servant."

God is so good and He gives us promises and keeps His promises. We have all known people in our lives that have made promises to us and not kept them. I have dealt with many people who are "stuck" in life because their father or someone significant broke their promises to them. The hurt they still bear can be debilitating! But God is good; He keeps His promises. As a matter of fact in 2 Corinthians 1:20 it says, "For all the promises of God in Him are Yes, and in Him Amen, to the glory of God through us." All the promises are Yes and Amen in Jesus!

I would like you to read this passage in The Message version. It is self-explanatory how good God is to David. He will be good to us too.

1 Chronicles 17:1-27, "After the king had made himself at home, he said to Nathan the prophet, 'Look at this: Here I am comfortable in a luxurious palace of cedar and the Chest of the Covenant of God sits under a tent.' 2 Nathan told David, 'Whatever is on your heart, go and do it; God is with you.' 3-6 But that night, the word of God came to Nathan, saying, 'Go and

tell my servant David, This is God's word on the matter: You will not build me a 'house' to live in. Why, I haven't lived in a 'house' from the time I brought up the children of Israel from Egypt till now; I've gone from one tent and makeshift shelter to another. In all my travels with all Israel, did I ever say to any of the leaders I commanded to shepherd Israel, 'Why haven't you built me a house of cedar?'

7-10 'So here is what you are to tell my servant David: The God-of-the-Angel-Armies has this word for you: I took you from the pasture, tagging after sheep, and made you prince over my people Israel. I was with you everywhere you went and mowed your enemies down before you; and now I'm about to make you famous, ranked with the great names on earth. I'm going to set aside a place for my people Israel and plant them there so they'll have their own home and not be knocked around anymore; nor will evil nations afflict them as they always have, even during the days I set judges over my people Israel. And finally, I'm going to conquer all your enemies.

10-14 'And now I'm telling you this: God himself will build you a house! When your life is complete and you're buried with your ancestors, then I'll raise up your child to succeed you, a child from your own body, and I'll firmly establish his rule. He will build a house to honor me, and I will guarantee his kingdom's rule forever. I'll be a father to him, and he'll be a son to me. I will never remove my gracious love from him as I did from the one who preceded you. I will set him over my house and my kingdom forever; his throne will always be there, rock solid.'

15 Nathan gave David a complete and accurate report of everything he heard and saw in the vision.

16-27 King David went in, took his place before God, and prayed: Who am I, my Master God, and what is my family, that you have brought me to this place in life? But that's nothing compared to what's coming, for you've also spoken of my family far into the future, given me a glimpse into tomorrow and looked on me, Master God, as a Somebody. What's left for David to say to this—to your honoring your servant, even though you know me, just as I am? O God, out of the goodness of your heart, you've taken your servant to do this great thing and put your great work on display.

There's none like you, God, no God but you, nothing to compare with what we've heard with our own ears. And who is like your people, like Israel, a nation unique on earth, whom God set out to redeem as his own people (and became most famous for it), performing great and fearsome acts, throwing out nations and their gods left and right as you saved your people from Egypt? You established for yourself a people—your very own Israel!—your people forever. And you, God, became their God.

So now, great God, this word that you have spoken to me and my family, guarantee it forever! Do exactly what you've promised! Then your reputation will be confirmed and flourish always as people exclaim, 'The God-of-the-Angel-Armies, the God over Israel, is Israel's God!' And the house of your servant David will remain rock solid under your watchful presence. You, my God, have told me plainly, 'I will build you a house.' That's how I was able to find the courage to pray this prayer to you.

God, being the God you are, you have spoken all these wonderful words to me. As if that weren't enough, you've blessed my family so that it will continue in your presence always. Because you have blessed it, God, it's really blessed—blessed for good!" (The Message).

## REFLECT AND RESPOND

Wow! God keeps His promises to the generations. He keeps His promises to us! Like David we can say, "Who am I, my Master God, and what is my family, that you have brought me to this place in life? But that's nothing compared to what's coming, for you've also spoken of my family far into the future, given me a glimpse into tomorrow and looked on me, Master God, as a Somebody. What's left for David to say to this - you're honoring your servant, even though you know me, just as I am?

O God, out of the goodness of your heart, you've taken your servant to do this great thing and put your great work on display."

God is with you! What promises has He given you? Pray over your promises.

RECEIVING THE GOODNESS OF GOD

# Day 20

Genesis 1:31, "Then God saw everything He had made and it was very good."

Let me chat with you for a moment about ricotta cheese. Now, stay with me because you simply have to know what a miracle happens when you combine milk, cream, salt, a tablespoon of vinegar or lemon juice and put it over heat. This is so easy that it must be wrong. No one is allowed to create something so delicious, so hip-expanding with one saucepan and a few stirs. All you have to do is assemble the ingredients and prepare to become a culinary all-star by barely lifting a finger.

Your first step is bringing the milk, cream and salt to a boil. Then stir in the vinegar and let the mixture volunteer to curdle for you while you pet the cat. Finally, dump the whole clumpy mess through a strainer lined with cheesecloth and eat a cookie or two while gravity does its drippy work. This takes a while, but it will be worth it. In an hour or less, voile'! You may not know the difference between a spatula and a sieve, but you are now the creator of fresh ricotta. You know, the stuff with the fancy Italian label you can pay six or seven dollars for in the deli. But this is so fresh that only the label and the moo are missing.

Your so-soft and creamy cheese can be drizzled with honey and topped with fresh fruit, spread on crackers with pepper and a drizzle of olive oil or made into unforgettable lasagna or pizza. It can even be eaten with a spoon while standing barefoot in front of the fridge with the door open. What a wonder. So simple, so elemental. And with apologies to the lactose-intolerant among us—so, so *good*.

Because this is a devotional and not a cookbook, let me tell you where I'm going with this. God isn't simple like ricotta, but oh, is He good! If it were possible to somehow break Him apart and send a sample to the lab for composition analysis, the report back would be sweet and simple. "No contaminants." You'd not find a milligram of meanness or malice in Him. Not a speck of selfishness or short-sightedness. Not a hint of hopelessness. God is pure, unadulterated goodness. That's as elemental as it gets.

If we, who are so flawed and prone to mess-ups, can still create something crazily good like ricotta with such ease, just imagine what God, who is purely, crazily, magnificently good, can create in and through us. And all without breaking a sweat.

## REFLECT AND RESPOND

What do you long for God to do in your life that would be "crazily good?" What can you do for God that would be "crazily good?"

*Lord, help me see creative possibilities today to partner with You in doing something "crazily good"!*

RECEIVING THE GOODNESS OF GOD

# Day 21

Galatians 5:22-23, "But the fruit of the Spirit is love, joy, peace, longsuffering, kindness, goodness, faithfulness, gentleness, self-control. Against such there is no law."

Goodness is a fruit of the Holy Spirit. The fruit of the Spirit grows in our life as we cooperate with God. God's goodness is different from "good works" to gain merit. It springs forth from the indwelling Spirit. Paul says in Romans 15:14, "Now I myself am confident concerning you, my brethren, that you also are full of goodness, filled with all knowledge, able also to admonish one another." We share God's goodness with one another. Our being good results in our doing good. Think of how you have received God's goodness through other people! God develops the fruit of the Spirit of goodness within us.

In Ephesians 5:8-10, Paul shares, "For you were once darkness, but now you are light in the Lord. Walk as children of light (for the fruit of the Spirit is in all goodness, righteousness, and truth), finding out what is acceptable to the Lord." In this context, Paul is teaching on light versus darkness. We should be walking opposite of the ways we did when we walked in darkness. As children of the light, let His goodness shine through you! Goodness is acceptable in the sight of the Lord.

What if the real inheritance that God wants us to covet are not land titles and precious metals? What if it is the fruit of the Spirit that grows deep within us? It is the secret to living the abundant life. It is defined as the ability to receive God's goodness and then share it with others. We have come to know the goodness of God, but it must not be hoarded. It must be shared.

## REFLECT AND RESPOND

How will you cooperate with the Holy Spirit to cultivate the fruit of goodness? Mediate on Galatians 5:22-23 and ask God.

RECEIVING THE GOODNESS OF GOD

# Day 22

Nehemiah 9:25, "And they took strong cities and a rich land, and possessed houses full of all goods, cisterns already dug, vineyards, olive groves, and fruit trees in abundance...and delighted themselves in Your great goodness."

Imagine living in 1862. Millions of acres of frontier land up for grabs by the thousands of settlers pouring into the Wild West. Plots of 200 acres selling for eighteen dollars each. (Now, that's a sale!) But wait, there's more. Before the "sod-busters" could call the land their own, they had to build a house on it, plant crops, and farm it—for five long years. I bet when the five-year mark rolled around, they had earned every spoon of that soil with sweat and sacrifice. They were entitled to that land—and then some.

Now imagine the Israelites flooding into the Promised Land, a land inherited through God's promise to old great-grandpa Abraham. They didn't pay even eighteen dollars. Unlike the sod-busters, they didn't face a howling prairie and barren acres of scrub, weeds and rocks. They didn't start from scratch, break the ground, build the houses, plant the crops, dig the wells. The work was already done for them in those "strong cities and rich lands." It was all ready and waiting.

The Israelites did fight for their land, but they weren't sod-busters. They were God-trusters. At least, they were learning to be. They weren't entitled to the land because of their hard labor; it was gifted to them, free and clear, by the God of abundance. Their response? Nehemiah tells us they "delighted themselves" in God. I can't help but notice that they didn't congratulate themselves: "We are awesome, brave and so totally deserving!" They delighted themselves. Their focus wasn't on their GPS skills, battle-readiness, or true grit. It was on God's great goodness.

Our culture seems a little long on deserving and a little short on delighting in God. Is it just me or have you noticed the constant barrage of media messages about how much more we all deserve—from a luxury car to a great-tasting soda, from instant banking to our "very best life." I even heard a weather forecaster this week promising clear, sunny skies and then adding, "And we all deserve this." Everyone on camera was smiling and nodding in agreement. Um, I didn't do a thing to deserve gorgeous weather. Did you? I'm so confused.

Between you and me, I'm thinking that the fastest route to delight (and to reality) is getting something we know full well we don't deserve and can never earn, like a cloudless day or say, God's love and forgiveness. One of the most amazing things about salvation? It cost Jesus everything and us absolutely nothing. It's a free gift, a house already built, a well already dug, a tree already planted and loaded with fruit.

But even as God-trusters, sometimes the old sod-buster in us can't quite take its hands off the plow. Surely if we pray longer, get angry less, witness more, all that effort will stake us just a little more claim to God's love. Thank heavens, life in God doesn't work like that. Trying to earn love dries up delight like the summer sun scorches the prairie. So hands off the plow for me. I'd rather just be blessed by my great and good God. And delighted!

## REFLECT AND RESPOND

Are you choosing to live as a spiritual "sod-buster" or as a "God-truster"?

How can you delight yourself today in the goodness God is freely giving you?

## RECEIVING THE GOODNESS OF GOD

# Day 23

Psalm 16:2, "O my soul, you have said to the Lord, 'You are my Lord, my goodness is nothing apart from You.'"

The Psalmist understood that our goodness is nothing apart from the Lord. I often say, "Any good thing you see in me is because of Him." He is so full of goodness. As a matter of fact, Psalm 33:5 says, "He loves righteousness and justice; the earth is full of the goodness of the Lord."

The word *goodness* in the Greek is "*agathosune*; i.e. virtue or beneficence, goodness. It comes from a root word that means an intrinsic goodness rather than an outward appearance!"[2]

We have a choice to live life seeing the goodness of the Lord and focusing on Him or seeing the evil and the darkness. Don't misunderstand! We all see evil in a fallen world, but we can BE GOOD NEWS if we focus our eyes, mind and heart on God and His goodness. The earth is full of the goodness of God. Look for it!

God wants His goodness to pour into you and out of you. We can be His goodness dispenser. When people push on us or squeeze us...goodness should come out. You can be a

2 The Spirit-Filled Life Bible, (NKJV), Thomas Nelson, Nashville, TN, Jack Hayford, General Editor footnote, (©2002), pg. 1573.

goodness dispenser in a world full of evil and darkness. People need to experience His goodness practically.

Goodness dispensed, is His fragrance, released from love, from God above!

## REFLECT AND RESPOND

How can you dispense His goodness today? Do you know someone who needs some goodness dispensed into their life?

RECEIVING THE GOODNESS OF GOD

# Day 24

Psalm 107:1, "Thank the Lord because He is good. His love continues forever."

Most of us know the old saying, "absence makes the heart grow fonder." I wonder: if God's goodness was suddenly gone, how long would it take us to notice?

### If God's Goodness Went Missing

Thank God for His goodness! Oh, where would we be
Were He to withhold it from you and from me?
No families. Or friendships. Or sheltering trees.
No feeling God's presence. Or finding lost keys.
No whispered I-love-yous or shouted amens.
No listening or learning or making amends.
Goodbye, work that matters, and dreams that inspire.
Goodbye, heaven's promise—no looking up higher.
No kids with the giggles. No meaningful glance.
No memories or mysteries. And no second chance.

No nose to hold glasses. No heroes to rise.

No roaring of oceans or star-glittered skies.

So long, celebrations, and any glad news.

Goodbye, noble causes. No power to choose.

So long to all thank-yous and uplifted prayer.

No sunsets or secrets or coffee to share.

No hope for the broken. No new trails to roam.

No stories to tell and nowhere to call home.

Thank God for His goodness! Oh, where would we be

Were He to withhold it from you and from me?

Poem by: Deena Wilson

## REFLECT AND RESPOND

What would you miss the most if God were to stop being good, stop showing His love in your life?

Take some time to praise Him that He's good 24/7 and His love continues forever.

## RECEIVING THE GOODNESS OF GOD

# Day 25

Jeremiah 31:14, "I will satiate the soul of the priests with abundance, and My people shall be satisfied with My goodness, says the Lord."

God is speaking to Israel in this passage about restoring them. He told them He had "loved them with everlasting love..." (Jeremiah 31:3). He loves us with an everlasting love. He loves us passionately. He had scattered Israel, but is gathering them back.

In Jeremiah 31:12 he says, "Therefore they shall come and sing in the height of Zion, streaming to the goodness of the Lord—for wheat and new wine and oil, for the young of the flock and the herd; their souls shall be like a well-watered garden, and they shall sorrow no more at all." We, too, can stream to the goodness of the Lord. He wants to make your soul (your mind, will and emotions) like a well-watered garden. My wife is very good at keeping our garden well-watered and the plants, trees, flowers and shrubs grow so beautifully. God wants to water you in this season to cause growth in your life. Will you let Him water you?

Jeremiah 31:14 says that God wants to satiate us or fill us to the full with His abundance. God is the God of abundance.

He wants to fill you with His abundance. God does abundance. God wants to satisfy us with His goodness. He wants to fill you to satisfaction! He wants to release His abundant supply to you. Get your loading dock ready; God is about to supply you with His abundant goodness!

## REFLECT AND RESPOND

How is God watering you right now? Is He using someone to water you? Why not ask them to pray for you? What part of your "garden" needs to be watered?

RECEIVING THE GOODNESS OF GOD

# Day 26

Acts 10:38, "…How God anointed Jesus of Nazareth with the Holy Spirit and with power, who went about doing good and healing all who were oppressed by the devil, for God was with Him.

Recently, as I wrestled through a hard time, a friend prayed for me that I would boldly "run to the battle line" as David did when he confronted Goliath (1 Samuel 17:48). I have to admit, I winced. And maybe gulped. A little. I'm not a wimp; I'm just sometimes a reluctant warrior. My claim to fame would not be rushing into battles, spiritual or otherwise. Unlike David, and unlike Jesus, who boldly went where no man had gone before, taking on darkness at every turn, I'm better on defense than offense. When it comes to conflict, I could take some very long lessons from Jesus, from David and even, believe it or not, from the lowly mantis shrimp.

Have you ever heard about him? Making his home in the warm waters of the Indian and Pacific Oceans, the mantis shrimp boasts an outsized confidence. At just two to seven inches long, this little creature seems to know exactly who he is. He's alert. He's armored. And he's armed.

No one's sneaking up on this guy, ever. His eyes, made up of millions of light-sensitive cells, are the most complex and alert in the animal kingdom. He can see ten times more color than you and me, including ultraviolet light. Using the shrimp's superb eye design as inspiration, medical researchers are now developing powerful cameras to pinpoint the tiniest cancer cells.

As a crustacean, the mantis shrimp's lobster-like, hard-shelled body is custom-made for repelling attacks. He's completely at home in his body armor. Fits him like a glove and he never takes it off. He's securely shielded 24/7. But his real wow factor is his startling punch.

His jackknife claws can spring and strike with the speed of a .22 caliber bullet— fifty times faster than the blink of an eye. One lightning blow can splinter a crab's shell, deck a much larger enemy, or even fracture the glass of an aquarium! No wonder he can "run to the battle line" of his shrimp life with such confidence. (Well, at least "run" as fast as six shrimpy legs can carry him.)

Here's what I'm thinking. God in His goodness has gone to extraordinary lengths to fully equip a mantis shrimp, a creature that will spend its entire life burrowing in ocean muck. So how much more will He equip me, the "crown of His creation?" I too am able to be keenly aware of my enemy, prowling around like a roaring lion, seeking the next soul or situation to devour. I too have available the full 24/7 mind and body armor of the Spirit: my shield of faith, breastplate of righteousness, helmet of salvation. Fits me like a glove. And by His power, I too can deliver some lightning strikes with impressive force, shattering darkness and evil and releasing the goodness of God into my world. As Paul reminds me, "The weapons of our warfare are not carnal, but mighty in God for pulling down strongholds" (2 Corinthians 10:4). So true. And so easy to forget.

Maybe for my own inspiration, I should set up a little aquarium at home with a mantis shrimp of my own. I could peer at him on days when I need courage and declare, "The two of us are awesomely alert, armored and armed by God to run to our battle lines!" I'm picky about names for my pets, though, and I might feel awkward calling my fellow warrior by his formal scientific name, odontodactylus scyallrus. So maybe I'd just nickname him: David.

## REFLECT AND RESPOND

Do you "run to the battle lines" in your life for God? Or are you better at defense than offense?

*Lord, as I live for You today, remind me that in any conflict I'm equipped by You to be alert, armored and armed to release Your goodness into my world!*

RELEASING THE GOODNESS OF GOD

# Day 27

Hebrews 6:4-6, "For it is impossible for those who were once enlightened, and have tasted the heavenly gift, and have become partakers of the Holy Spirit, and have tasted the good word of God and the powers of the age to come, if they fall away, to renew them again to repentance, since they crucify again for themselves the Son of God, and put Him to an open shame."

The writer of Hebrews is giving a stern warning in these verses to not fall away from God and crucify again the Son of God, and put Him to an open shame. This amazing passage lists the incredible ways we have seen and tasted the goodness of God.

We, who have a relationship with Jesus Christ have been enlightened. We have come out of darkness into His marvelous light. We have tasted of the heavenly gift. We have received Christ as our Lord and Savior. How good is that! We have partaken of the Holy Spirit. I am a Spirit-filled believer enjoying fellowship with the Holy Spirit. We have tasted the good word of God. How rich the word of God is to us who know Christ is speaking to us. We have tasted of the powers of the age to come. I have seen God speak to people's hearts, heal many, save people, baptize many with water and the Holy Spirit and speak to people's hearts. I have had the privilege of traveling to many nations and seeing people taste the power of the age to come—the supernatural power of the Holy Spirit.

When you have tasted and seen God's goodness in all these ways, you want <u>to release it</u>! How are we releasing the power of God? On one trip to Africa, I saw God open 13 deaf ears and nine blind eyes. God is so good! You can release God's goodness and love to people all around the world! If you see the goodness of God, you can receive the goodness of God and release the goodness of God.

## REFLECT AND RESPOND

How is God challenging you to release His goodness? Well, what are you waiting for...do it!

# Releasing the Goodness of God

## RELEASING THE GOODNESS OF GOD

# Day 28

Lamentations 3:25, "The Lord is good to those who wait for Him, to the soul who seeks Him."

My young friend, Todd, is looking for Jesus. He just doesn't know it. Yet. We've been friends a while now and I know some of his wanderings and wounds. I also know that for a long time God was nowhere on his radar. He didn't want God, didn't need him. To Todd, God was beyond uncaring or powerless or missing in action; He was non-existent. He was a concept, an imagination maybe, but not a reality. My heart has ached for Todd. I've done my best to listen, share my faith, be a real friend, love's hands and feet to him.

One day while I was praying (and I'm not even sure I was praying for Todd), a quick picture flashed into my mind. I don't put much stock in experiences or impressions like this unless they line up with the spirit and truth of the Bible. But when they do, then the Holy Spirit has my attention. In this picture, I saw Todd, standing with his back to me. He looked strong, feet solidly planted, arms crossed. He was facing a large open-air market, with striped tent awnings, vendors booths stacked with merchandise, sawdust-covered aisles. I sensed that the Holy Spirit was whispering to my heart, "He's in the marketplace of ideas and beliefs." I felt my adrenaline buzzing. Finally! It seemed

Todd was going shopping, not for tires or jeans, but for the kingdom of God. Which is really biblical, if you read Matthew 13:45 where Jesus describes the search for His kingdom as the ultimate shopping trip. My hopes were up that Todd would give his heart to Jesus soon.

But my excitement was short-lived. I guess I was expecting Todd to do spiritually what I might call typical "guy-shopping"–a beeline for the needed item and back out the door like a shot. But instead, he began methodically exploring the world's religions one by one in great detail. What? This wasn't at all bee-like and not according to plan (at least not mine.) It seemed every time I saw Todd, his nose was in a new book about how to find enlightenment and truth. If he was going to wade through the entire alphabet soup of beliefs, what if he got stuck on Buddhism or humanism or Islam and never even made it to the J for Jesus? In other words, what if he swallowed the lies, got misled? One day I was urgently explaining all this to God (just so He too would realize this might be a major problem). And right in the middle of my prayer, another picture popped to mind.

I saw Todd in the "marketplace of beliefs" again, but this time he wasn't alone. Jesus was standing right beside him, shoulder to shoulder. And looking closer, I saw that Jesus had also stationed Himself beside every vendor's booth! My gut feeling was that there that is absolutely no way Jesus is going to let Todd miss seeing Him. Lamentations 3:25 promises, "The Lord is good to those who wait for him, to the soul who seeks him." Jesus is big enough to stick faithfully with Todd, no matter how broken or circuitous his path to Him is, no matter how long it takes. Hallelujah for a God whose goodness is so great that He protects and honors the heart sincerely searching for Him.

My part for now? It's to keep the prayers for Todd flowing, keep the faith conversations and questions going, keep the friendship growing. And when Todd does come to Jesus? My guess is he's going to have an awesome real-world faith, well-considered and chosen, as solid and immoveable as a brick wall. He's going to know exactly what he believes, Whom he loves and why. God can always use a man like that.

## REFLECT AND RESPOND

Do you have a "Todd", a non-Christian friend or family member, in your life now? Can you do one thing today to show them God's goodness?

If you have no non-Christian friends, are you willing to ask God to guide you in finding one?

RELEASING THE GOODNESS OF GOD

# Day 29

2 Chronicles 6:41, "Now therefore, arise, O Lord God, to Your resting place, You and the ark of Your strength. Let Your priests, O Lord God, be clothed with salvation, and let Your saints rejoice in goodness."

This is part of Solomon's prayer in 2 Chronicles 6. Solomon had built the house of the Lord. The temple was dedicated to the Lord. There are many key verses in this prayer. One is 2 Chronicles 6:14, "And he said, 'Lord God of Israel, there is no God in heaven or on earth like You, who keep Your covenant and mercy with Your servants who walk before You with all their hearts." A second key verse is 2 Chronicles 6:30, "Then hear from heaven, Your dwelling place, and forgive, and give to everyone according to all his ways, whose heart You know (for You alone know the hearts of the sons of men)." God keeps covenant like no God in heaven or on earth and He knows our hearts!

In this passage Solomon is asking God to take possession of the temple and make it His resting place. He asks God to make the temple a place of service where the priests are clothed with salvation and the saints rejoice in goodness. Solomon wanted the saints to rejoice in the goodness of God. We can make a choice to rejoice in the goodness of God.

As New Testament saints, we can receive the goodness of God. If we have received the goodness of God, we can rejoice in God's goodness. God's presence is full of goodness. Let God surround you with His goodness. His goodness can affect you and infect you! Are you glad about the good things God is doing? Remember He knows your heart! Let Him fill you full of His goodness! Receive it now!

## REFLECT AND RESPOND

Just as Solomon asked God to fill the temple and make it His resting place, God wants to fill us, His temple, today. He wants us to be filled with salvation and goodness. He not only wants us to receive His goodness, but REJOICE in His goodness. Go ahead and tell Him: *Lord, I receive Your goodness and now I want to rejoice in it!*

RELEASING THE GOODNESS OF GOD

# Day 30

Acts 14:17, "Nevertheless He did not leave Himself without witness, in that He did good, gave us rain from heaven and fruitful seasons, filling our hearts with food and gladness."

My doctor once wrote me a playful prescription, "Vacation in a sunny, warm location." The drippy, gray Seattle winters can leave me feeling that I'm either growing moss between my toes or rusting. I need my sunlamp, tropical fruit, my cheerful steel drum music so I can at least pretend my friend, the sun, is close by. Until recently, pretending to be in the sun was about all the good people in Rjukan, Norway could do.

Rjukan has been in the news a lot in the last several years. The little town's claim to fame is that it has finally stepped into the sun after a century in shadows. Rjukan sits on the floor of a deep valley, between the shoulders of sun-blocking mountains. Spectacular scenery looking up, I bet, when it's light enough to see it. It used to be that for a full six months of the year, the town was covered in shadows. Uggh. Six months of darkness? The brave souls of Rjukan make me look like a real weather wimp.

But everything changed in the little town in the winter of 2013. If they hadn't known what was coming, I can imagine the 2,400 pale citizens shielding their eyes from the brightness, pointing skyward, and saying, "What on earth is *that*?" as sunlight came beaming down for the first time into the town square. It would have felt like some sort of visitation or maybe an enormous spotlight or just a miracle after so many bleak, black winters.

The sun's appearance didn't catch them by surprise though. Everybody in town would have seen and heard the helicopters coming in, lifting three 538-foot solar mirrors into place on one of the mountains. Precisely placed and computer-controlled, the mirrors are now busily tracking the sun as it moves. They turn, tilt, rotate. They make it their sole mission to reflect that sunny glow down onto Rjukan. Now the library is lit up, the town hall, the tourist office. There are new benches for soaking up some rays. People congregate; chatting happens. Moms push along strollers, kids run in circles, cats appear on windowsills. The grateful townspeople say it's amazing, that this is the light that they've longed for.

I guess we don't have to be in Norway to appreciate that there can be a lot of sun-obstructing mountains in our lives too. And sun-starved people aren't only in Rjukan. When I see a homeless veteran panhandling at the freeway exit or hold my friend as she cries over losing her mom or watch coverage of the latest war, famine, or natural disaster, I'm reminded. In some senses, we all live on—or make visits to—the floor of a valley. The winter shadows of pain and fear, loss and hopelessness threaten to swallow us all at times.

Yet Jesus promises, "…I am the light of the world. He who follows Me shall not walk in darkness, but shall have the light of life"(John 8:12). And then He calls out the major mirror factor in all of us who are following Him. "You are the light of the world" (Matthew 5:14). We are the hand-crafted, Spirit-led, Jesus-tracking reflectors of God's life-giving light. We move when He moves. We turn when He turns. We're the giant mirrors He has lovingly placed in just the right families, jobs, neighborhoods, schools. We've been positioned in cultures, callings and circles of influence to send His sun shooting into shadows.

Funny, isn't it? At first glance, we appear to just be soccer moms, accountants, cousins, construction workers, neighbors, retirees or the average family going about everyday life. But in reality? We're like those massive, mighty mirrors of Rjukan. We're warming a winter world, beaming God's goodness to every single corner where the sun doesn't shine.

## REFLECT AND RESPOND

*Jesus, help me really see the people I meet today. Remind me that I don't know the shadows they may live in or the load they may be carrying. Help me be intentional about reflecting You and Your goodness to everyone I meet.*

RELEASING THE GOODNESS OF GOD

# Day 31

Psalm 68:10, "Your congregation dwelt in it; You, O God, provided from Your goodness for the poor."

In Psalm 68 David is talking about taking the Ark of the Covenant to Mount Zion. It starts with verse 1, "Let God arise, let His enemies be scattered; let those also who hate Him flee before Him." There is so much in this amazing psalm, but I would like to concentrate on verse 10. God is speaking to the congregation of Israel in Psalm 68.

God has a special place in His heart for the poor. Verse 10 says, "…You, O God, provided from Your goodness for the poor." The Bible says a lot about the poor. In Proverbs 21:13, "Whoever shuts their ears to the cry of the poor will also cry out and not be answered" (NIV). Proverbs 29:7, "The righteous considers the cause of the poor, but the wicked does not understand such knowledge." Proverbs 14:21 says, "He who despises his neighbor sins; but he who has mercy on the poor, happy is he." In Galatians 2:10, Paul says, "They desired only that we should remember the poor, the very thing which I also was eager to do." May we be eager to remember the poor.

God's goodness needs to be released to the poor. I want to encourage you to ask God to show you someone who is poor that He might want you to bless. There are many people in need. As we give to those in need, God says we will be happy! Have a Happy Day by helping somebody in need. God's goodness is to be shown to the poor. When we release His goodness by giving to the poor, we make God happy too! Let God's goodness pour out of you to the poor.

## REFLECT AND RESPOND

How can you release God's goodness to the poor? Ask Him!

RELEASING THE GOODNESS OF GOD

# Day 32

2 Thessalonians 3:13, "But as for you, brethren, do not grow weary in doing good."

I was surprised to see the unfamiliar blue van in my driveway and the pretty Asian teenager at my front door. Her smile was as bright as her English was halting. "Your bush? I can cut?" She was waving a small pair of green garden clippers, motioning eagerly toward our side yard where our big forsythia bush was overhanging the fence.

"Um…" I stepped out into the chill on the front porch with her, confused. The forsythia didn't seem like a cause for such excitement. It was a tangled mess of dead wood, its bone-like branches spiking up into the dull January sky. It took me a few moments and a consultation with her older sister waiting in the van to understand their mission. Crunching through gravel and dead leaves, I led them around our house to what was, in their eyes, the bush of promise. The sister reached up, gently pulling a branch toward us.

"See here?" She pointed to the tight little pairs of brown knots—bud wannabes—dotting its length. "Warm water and two weeks." She smiled and began to confidently clip, evaluating branches as she went with a practiced eye. In two weeks, she assured me, their mother's house would be full of beautiful flowers, coaxed into early golden bloom. This was exactly the beauty they needed, just in time for their Chinese New Year celebration.

In a few moments they drove away, exhilarated and laughing, unpromising-looking branches heaped in their back seat. I gathered up the bundle I'd asked them to cut for me, pulled out my tall vase, filled it with warm water and branches, and set it on my entryway table. Blossoms in two weeks? Really? In the middle of winter? I was dubious. But then, winter has a way of doing that to me.

Oh, life's wintry places! Those times when talents or callings seem to lie dormant. Or anxieties multiply. Or hopes collide with reality. Circumstances don't cooperate and neither do people. We find that kids aren't really grown up at 18 (who came up with that myth?) and the mirror announces that wrinkling happens a good decade before we expect it. We'd like a little more appreciation, a whole lot more vacation. Putting one foot in front of the other can be daunting. We're just plain tired.

Yet the apostle Paul urges us not to give up on doing good. I don't believe for a minute that he's saying be superhuman: don't wrestle, don't rest, don't recharge and renew. I just think he's reminding us not to let winter-weariness or bud-blindness have the final say. It's almost as if Paul is standing on the front porch of our lives, smiling and waving his garden clippers. Keep on keeping on, he encourages us, because quietly, invisibly— and inevitably—frozen ground begins thawing if we don't give up. Whether that ground is a sulky teenager, a broken heart or body, an elusive dream, a pile of bills, or a sin-sick world.

In a couple weeks, lo and behold! My entryway was boasting a gorgeous spray of golden forsythia blooms. They were a daily reminder to me that it matters to hang onto hope. We just never know the exact tipping point when brownness and brittleness will surrender to budding and blooming. It could be just a little warm water and two weeks away.

## REFLECT AND RESPOND

Micah 7:7 reads, "But as for me, I will watch expectantly for the Lord, I will wait for the God of my salvation" (NASB). Is this your declaration of faith today?

*Lord, help me keep on doing good as I trust You for break-throughs for myself and others. Even though I may not yet see any "blooms", by faith I thank You that I will!*

RELEASING THE GOODNESS OF GOD

# Day 33

James 1:17, "Every good gift and every perfect gift is from above, and comes down from the Father of lights, with whom there is no variation or shadow of turning."

God is a good God! God is full of goodness. He gives good gifts. I love to watch people discover the gifts that God has given them, then watch them develop and deploy them. As a pastor, I have great joy watching people be equipped and then use their spiritual gifts to positively affect many people.

In 1 Peter 4:10, "As each one has received a gift, minister it to one another, as good stewards of the manifold grace of God." We are to administer our gifts as "good" stewards. Stewards are managers of another's household. We are managers in God's household to use the gifts He has given us to bless and encourage others. We are to minister to one another. You and I release God's goodness when we exercise the gifts He has given to us. You are gifted with good gifts from God the Father to release love, grace and truth to people.

God is the source of goodness. God only gives good gifts... NO BAD ONES! His gifts are an extension of His goodness which He has given to men and women. How has God gifted you?

What are you doing with the good gifts He has given you? How are you investing in those gifts?

Everyone gets gifts from God. Each gift is so personal and useful that no one is left out. 1 Corinthians 12:1 says, "Now concerning spiritual gifts, brethren, I do not want you to be ignorant." Let's release God's goodness by using our spiritual gifts to bless people. You can make a difference.

## REFLECT AND RESPOND

What gifts has God given you? How are you managing them? Ask God who He wants you to minister to and release His goodness.

RELEASING THE GOODNESS OF GOD

# Day 34

Psalm 31:19, "Oh, how great is Your goodness…which You have prepared for those who trust in You in the presence of the sons of men!"

God so loves to show His goodness to the "sons (and daughters) of men." If you have a son, I wonder if your experience has been anything like mine. In their growing-up years, if my guys spotted an incoming hug from Mom, they reacted as if they were about to be injected with flesh-eating bacteria. I could have taken this personally and sometimes I did. But I learned to soldier on forward with the hugging, even as they grew older, because I love them to the moon and back and because this is what mom's do.

But with the years I've refined my hugging approach. Now I creep up from behind when they're unsuspecting and preoccupied, quickly wrap my arms around their impressive shoulders and squeeze. I don't linger (much) and it's all over before they know it, like a flu shot or payroll deductions. This method works well, almost always.

It's good, I think, to have a multitude of ways to say, "I love you". Hugging alone just doesn't cut it. Multi-layered affection is what's needed. I used to follow my guys to the front door as they left for work or school. I'd flip on the porch light for them, wave and call out, "Love you! Have a good day!" or some variation of that. Maybe they were far too old for this. Maybe I just didn't see them sighing and rolling their eyes. I don't know. I just have this near-ridiculous belief in the power of small acts of love like this.

One day I flipped on our porch light as usual as my younger son strode past me to meet his high school world, loaded down with his laptop, sax, backpack. My finger may have even still been on the light switch when a memory from my own young adulthood blinked on inside me. I remembered my dad, standing at our front door, waving as I backed my car down the driveway. The door would close and then our porch light would blink off and then on again, like a winking yellow eye. Once, twice, maybe three times. Those blinks meant, "Bye! Be safe! We love you!"

So guess what? The porch light at our house sometimes began blinking on and off too. I filled my guys in on the porch light family story, so they would know the blinking light didn't just mean bum wiring. It means just the same thing now as it did years ago when Dad stood at the door for me, watching me begin to slowly pull away. "Bye! Be safe! We love you!" Even the young adult sons and daughters of men can use a little touch of love and legacy like that.

## REFLECT AND RESPOND

In what ways does God show His daily love and care for you?

Can you show love today in one new way to someone you care about?

## RELEASING THE GOODNESS OF GOD

# Day 35

Romans 12:21, "Do not be overcome by evil, but overcome evil with good."

I believe we can see the goodness of God, receive the goodness of God and release the goodness of God. We live in a world full of evil and a world full of the goodness of God. We are overcomers and we can overcome evil.

Revelation 12:11,12 says, "And they overcame him by the blood of the Lamb and by the word of their testimony, and they did not love their lives to the death. Therefore rejoice, O heavens, and you who dwell in them! Woe to the inhabitants of the earth and the sea! For the devil has come down to you, having great wrath, because he knows that he has a short time." We overcome evil and the evil one with God! Yes, the devil is evil and wrathful, but God's goodness overcomes evil and the evil one!

One of my heroes is William Wilberforce, who was converted to Christ in 1784-85. His saying was, "Let's make goodness fashionable." He did this himself by doing good in many ways and pushing back evil in England. Wilberforce worked tirelessly to abolish the transatlantic slave trade. He was also involved in at least 70 other philanthropic projects. By doing good throughout his life, Wilberforce reformed the morals of England. What are some of the ways we can "make goodness fashionable?"

There are many issues we can pray about and get involved with in today's world: drugs, alcohol, human trafficking, homelessness and the list goes on! We can make a difference by letting God's love and goodness flow through us!

## REFLECT AND RESPOND

*Lord, help me make "goodness fashionable." Show me where You want me to bring Your goodness in the midst of evil.*

Release His goodness and watch evil get overwhelmed and overcome!

RELEASING THE GOODNESS OF GOD

# Day 36

2 Kings 7:9, "Then they said to one another, 'We are not doing right. This is a day of good news, and we remain silent… come, let us go and tell the king's household.'"

There seem to be about a million and one reasons not to speak up when a voice is needed. And all of the reasons seem pretty, well, reasonable. I'm tired. Surely someone else is better qualified to say or do something. I might be misunderstood. Disliked. Laughed at. (Or worse.) I don't have time right now. I have more than enough on my plate. Who, me??

And if we can't convince ourselves with our full buffet of reasons to stuff it, it seems someone else can always supply plenty of extra reasons for us. "Dude, stop going to Pharaoh." the Israelites pleaded with Moses, "You're making things worse, not better." (In other words, keep the status quo, even if it stinks.) "No more praying to that God of yours," the government officials warned Daniel, "it's majorly illegal." (Challenging authority? Deadly idea.) "Shut up," the people in the crowd told blind Bartemaeus as he hollered for Jesus' attention. (Don't make a scene.) "Be quiet," the religious leaders threatened Peter and John. "We forbid you to speak of this Jesus anymore." (Very bad things happen to troublemakers and boat-rockers.)

But then there's King Solomon, a wise guy in the most authentic way. "...There is a time to be quiet," he counsels us in Ecclesiastes 3:7, "and a time to speak." And what about those four skinny lepers in 2 Kings 7? Doomed to die, they stumbled onto a feast and unimaginable booty in an abandoned enemy camp. I can imagine them all deliriously chowing down until maybe one of them burped loudly and had a personal ah-ha moment. Maybe he was waving a big roasted turkey leg as he said slowly, "Uh, guys? Something about all this doesn't feel quite–I don't know–*right*. How can we keep quiet about this find? I mean, when our friends back home are starving?" It took them awhile, but they decided good news was worth sharing.

And then there's Jesus. He said, "What I tell you in the dark speak in the daylight, what is whispered in your ear, proclaim from the roofs!" (Matthew 10:27 NIV). Well, so much for stuffing it. As Jesus-lovers, maybe you and I need to dare to ask ourselves, What about me? We've heard the greatest good news of all, so can we really keep quiet when:

A marriage needs the truth spoken in love.

A new neighbor needs a "hi".

A drifting teenager needs a boundary.

A school board needs the input of a concerned parent.

A government representative needs the voice of
the represented.

A stranger needs a welcome.

A victim needs a protector.

A worthy cause needs a champion.

A loving God needs a living witness.

The greatest good news ever told needs a proclaimer.

## REFLECT AND RESPOND

*Jesus, show me when to speak up and when to stay quiet. I can't speak up for everyone, but I can speak up for someone. Give me courage to find my voice and use it for goodness and for Your kingdom.*

RELEASING THE GOODNESS OF GOD

# Day 37

Nehemiah 2:18, "And I told them of the hand of my God which had been good upon me, and also of the king's words that he had spoken to me. So they said, 'Let us rise up and build.' Then they set their hands to this good work."

Nehemiah had a sad countenance and King Artaxerxes wondered why. Nehemiah was the king's cupbearer. He told the king he was sad because Jerusalem was in ruins and he wanted it to be restored. King Artaxerxes granted Nehemiah's request to give letters to the governors beyond the river. He also commanded Asaph, the keeper of the king's forest, to give Nehemiah timber to make beams for the broken-down gates. The king granted his requests because the good hand of God was upon Nehemiah.

Like Nehemiah, I see cities in ruin. I am asking King Jesus to guide us in raising up His Goodness Army in our area and around the world. I believe God's good hand is upon us to do it. He will supply the materials we need to build His Kingdom with His goodness. Like Nehemiah, I hope people will rise up and build His Kingdom as members of the Goodness Army. We will take His love and goodness out of the church into the city. His goodness needs to leave the building. Will you rise up and build with the Goodness Army?

The people set their hands to work in Nehemiah's day. Jesus set His hands to work in John 17. In verse four Jesus said, "I have glorified You on the earth. I have finished the work which You have given Me to do." We glorify God on earth by finishing the work He has given us to do! Do you know the work He has given you to do? Do it! Or ask Him to show you where you can join Him in His work.

Nehemiah raised up a "Goodness Army" that rebuilt the city of Jerusalem in 52 days. I believe God is raising up a Goodness Army you can be a part of today!

## REFLECT AND RESPOND

*Lord, show me my part in the army. I am reporting for duty. I will arise and build Your Kingdom. I thank You that You will provide the resources needed for the work You have called me to do.*

RELEASING THE GOODNESS OF GOD

# Day 38

Psalm 23:6, "Surely goodness and mercy shall follow me all the days of my life; and I will dwell in the house of the Lord forever."

Her name is Lillian Weber and I first read about her last year in an article by Lauren Blanchard for FoxNews.com. Lillian was just eight years old when she first began learning to sew her own little dresses. Today—over nine decades later—she's still sewing and really knows her way around spools of thread and stitches and seams. Amazingly, Lillian still makes most of her own clothes, and she'd probably be quite happy to show you she can even thread the needle by herself.

You never would have guessed that Lillian, at age 99, would become something of a "sewing celebrity". You can't miss her name on the webpage of Little Dresses for Africa, a Michigan-based Christian ministry. Providing simple, homemade dresses to girls in poverty, the ministry's mission is "to plant in the hearts of little girls that they are worthy." That's where Lillian comes in. In three years, she stitched and donated nearly 900 little dresses. But she didn't stop there. She also dreamed up quite a birthday challenge for herself. By May 5, 2015—when Lillian turned 100 years old—she hoped to have sewn her 1,000th dress for needy little girls she's never met.

"It's almost unreal of what I've made at my age, but my fingers are good, I can sew, I can thread," said Lillian. "I sit here once in a while and I sing a song to myself." I bet there's a lot Lillian can't do these days. I bet she's had some assorted aches and pains, and at least one or two very good reasons to just sit and watch the world go by. But she didn't have time to worry about things like that when she had at least 100 more little dresses to design and sew by May, for heaven's sake. She wanted each dress to be well-made and unique: a bow here, a pretty flower there, a snippet of lace on that pocket. The story of her birthday goal went viral while Lillian kept on sewing. And in March, two months early, she put the final stitch in her 1,000th little dress.

If you sat down and talked to Lillian today, she'd probably say simply as she has before, "I feel the good Lord has given me this to do." She's passionate about her sewing mission and says her accomplished goal isn't a finale. She keeps right on stitching her little dresses every day on a new sewing machine donated by Singer. My guess is that Lillian might just step over into heaven someday, her sewing scissors still in her pocket, her pincushion in hand and a new pattern in progress on her table.

Lillian could use some partners willing to donate funds to help ship her dresses to Africa. If you'd like to help, visit the Little Dresses for Africa website (www.littledressesforafrica.org) where you'll be reminded: "We're not just sending dresses, we're sending hope."

On May 5th, Lillian ordered a birthday breakfast of pancakes with strawberries and pored over her 400 cards from all around the world. It would have been hard to fit enough candles on a birthday cake for this amazing lady. But if someone tried, you can be sure that those 100 candles could never glow as brightly as the eyes and smiles of 1,000 little girls, twirling in pretty new dresses in the African sun.

## REFLECT AND RESPOND

At almost 100 years old, Lillian joined her heart to Little Dresses for Africa's mission of "changing the world, one little dress at a time". What has God, in His goodness, put in your heart to do for Him? Are you using the gifts He's given you for His kingdom?

RELEASING THE GOODNESS OF GOD

# Day 39

Acts 10:38, "How God anointed Jesus of Nazareth with the Holy Spirit and with power, who went about doing good and healing all who were oppressed by the devil, for God was with Him."

God the Father and His Son, Jesus, love to minister to people by doing good and healing all those oppressed by the devil. He was anointed to do this because God was with Him. God wants to be with us and anoint us like Jesus to do good and heal those oppressed by the devil. God wants to work with us and through us.

One time I was on an outreach team in Tanzania with Leif Hetland from Global Mission Awareness. In the afternoon we handed out flyers from the crusade we would be helping with in Dar es Salaam that night. I had a bad attitude, wondering why I had to be tripping through the mud and filth to try and talk to people who spoke a different language than mine. The Lord spoke to my heart and said, "You are doing this because I did this as I walked through cities and villages." I had to repent and ask God to forgive my attitude.

Then I saw a beautiful sidewalk right in the middle of the mud and filth and my thought, *"What is this doing here?"* The Lord spoke and said, "This is like My goodness." The sidewalk led us to a beauty shop. A Muslim woman and her friend came out of the shop and asked us to pray for her deaf daughter. When a group of us began to pray in Jesus' name, she was healed! The family came to the crusade that night and gave their lives to Jesus Christ. In spite of my bad attitude, which I had to repent of quickly, God saved people's lives. We went home with an attitude to go to the villages and cities to release His goodness!

## REFLECT AND RESPOND

You have been anointed just like Jesus was anointed. Jesus wants to release God's goodness and healing through you! Ask God how!

RELEASING THE GOODNESS OF GOD

# Day 40

1 Chronicles 16:34, "Oh, give thanks to the Lord, for He is good. For His mercy endures forever."

I always love "wrapping things up with a bow"...whether I'm readying a gift, finishing a good meal, or closing a letter to a friend. So let me offer a few final thoughts on how incredibly good God is. How I love Him! What a joy it is to be His forever!

## With A God Who Is Good

Oh, the things that you'll do,

With a God Who is good!

He invites you to join Him.

And really, you should.

You don't need a passport;

He won't charge a fee.

You just need to say yes.

And yeses are free!

All the landscape looks new,
With a God who is kind.
And you'll find yourself thinking,
"My, have I been blind?
With God's 'goodness glasses',
I see so much hope!
I'm NOT going to give up.
No, never! No, nope!

There are people to love;
There are prayers to pray.
There are wonders to wonder.
I'm starting today!
I CAN make a difference.
I WILL bless my world!
My sword is uplifted;
My banner unfurled!"

Oh, the way your heart shapes
With a God Who is good,
Growing bigger and softer
Than you thought it could.
It glows with a glowing;
It opens its doors.
And deep from the inside,
God's goodness just pours.

No, there's no holding back
What God's love is about.
And you won't find an "off" switch
On His goodness spout.
The more that you pour out,
The fuller you'll feel.
God's goodness is endless.
And realer than real.

Oh, the things that you'll do,
With a God Who is good.
He invites you to join Him.
And really, you could.
You don't need a passport;
He won't charge a fee.
You just need to say yes.
And yeses are free!

Poem by: Deena Wilson

## REFLECT AND RESPOND

May you live today—and every day—in the love and goodness of God!

## CLOSING SALVATION INVITATION

If you would like to receive Jesus Christ as your Lord and Savior, you can pray this prayer right now:

Dear God the Father,

I confess I am a sinner and need your forgiveness. I believe Jesus Christ, your Son died in my place on the cross and paid the penalty for my sin. And I believe Jesus rose from the dead. I repent and turn from sin and accept Jesus Christ as my personal Lord and Savior. I commit my life to you God and ask that the Holy Spirit would take control and help me live the Christian life. Than you for loving and accepting me as your child God. In Jesus Name, Amen.

If you have prayed this prayer from your heart and became God's child, please contact me at danhammerministries@isonrise.org.

## CONTACT INFORMATION

How has God blessed you through this devotional? We'd love to hear from you! Please send your praise reports, comments or questions to: danhammerministries@isonrise.org.

To purchase additional copies of this devotional or The Goodness of God by Dr. Dan C. Hammer: bookstore@isonrise.org.

For information about the developing Sonrise Goodness Army: goodnessarmy@isonrise.org.

To contact Dr. Dan C. Hammer: danhammerministries@isonrise.org.

To contact Deena Wilson or purchase her book, *A Mom's Legacy*: wilsondeena@gmail.com.

For general information about the ministries of Sonrise Christian Center: www.isonrise.org and or info@isonrise.org.

## ABOUT THE AUTHOR

Deena feels blessed to belong to the Sonrise family. She writes to celebrate the amazing God of hope and to inspire others to joyfully journey with Him. She is an engaging speaker, storyteller, teacher, poet and "toucher of hearts." Deena is the author of A Mom's Legacy: Five Simple Ways to say Yes to What Counts Forever. She and her husband, Alex, have two awesome young adult sons.

Deena feels like a rich woman when she's taking long walks, having good talks, asking honest questions or finding beauty in unexpected places.

## FROM PASTOR DAN

Deena Wilson is a gifted woman of God. Deena is a wife to Alex and mother to Chandler and Ethan. She loves her family very much. She has an incredible writing gift. I call her a "female Max Lucado." She has a great ability to tell stories that weave God's truth into a tale that speaks to your heart.

I have known her for over 30 years. She has a tremendous commitment to Jesus Christ and His Kingdom. She is also a gifted teacher and speaker.

## ABOUT THE AUTHOR

Dr. Dan C. Hammer is a servant leader and a visionary with a passion to reach people with The Gospel of Jesus Christ. He loves to equip the saints to do the work of the ministry. Dan is the President of Seattle Bible College, Chancellor of Wagner Leadership Institute Seattle and a member of the United States Coalition of Apostolic Leaders. He has ministered in many nations.

He has a Bachelor of Theology from Seattle Bible College and a Masters and Doctorate from Bakke Graduate University.

Dan and his wife Terry planted Sonrise Christian Center in 1986 and are the senior pastors there in Everett, Washington. They have two grown married sons and a grown daughter. They have five grandchildren and live in Everett, Washington.

## FROM DEENA WILSON

Pastor Dan and Terry have been my pastors for over twenty years. I'm thankful beyond words for both of them. Probably no one has spoken into my life more consistently, Sunday after Sunday, about the love, goodness and father-heart of God than Pastor Dan. Through the years, I've been freed and deeply shaped by his faithful teaching of God's Word and by the humble, passionate way he and Terry are honoring and following Jesus.

It's a privilege to partner with Pastor Dan in writing this devotional. He's given me great creative liberty to celebrate God's goodness in original, unexpected ways. Very fun!

Pastor Dan and Terry are such reminders to me of God's great goodness. They always make me want to love Jesus more. How blessed I am by the gift of their love and leadership in my life!

Made in the USA
Charleston, SC
29 October 2015